PARK BENCH
PHILOSOPHER

Park Bench Philosopher

JD Vail

FREEAIR Books

Contents

Awareness

suspend belief
to find
truth
what exists in this moment
outside the peripheral
is just noise
consumerism is noise
religion is noise
politics is noise
so, settle for the tune reverberating
in the mind
the noise of one's own creation
no Instragram needed

Latchkey Kid

raised by television
MTV
VH1
raised by drugs
alcohol
porn
raised by a loving mother
and a wayward father
I've lost contact with my sister
I stopped speaking to my brother years ago
my parents died years ago
loneliness finds me
as I sleepwalk
in and out of dive bars
holding onto loneliness
tight
never letting go

Honoring Death

inside a funeral home
salty tears
gather
to warm the soul

The Self

we've been at war
for nearly 20 years
going back and forth
dreaming up personalities
and burying them just as quickly
we fight
claw
scratch
stab each other
in the back
I struggle to find the way back
to loving myself
so, I've learned to compromise
a constant give and take
compromise on big decisions
like binge drinking today
so I can watch porn
tomorrow

Found

you can search for years
and not find yourself
you can put on clothes
take them off
and put on a new mask
you can find "the one"
you can make her cum multiple times in 15 minutes
and ride around in million-dollar cars
but
you can still come up
empty
you can still feel as life is draining you dry
like a large boil
on the inner thigh
and after the draining
the infection remains
so, you drain it again
and again
and again
but
until you tap into the infection
and live through the pain
you won't find what has been hiding all along:
everything you need to be
in your most vulnerable

form

Fetch Me My Old Man Clothes

anyone read Bukowski anymore?
or Sylvia Plath?
Raymond Carver?
of course not
too fringe
not politically correct
too broken
spiritually
culturally
mentally
they didn't pass the purity test
no DEI training
I'm sitting in a hipster ramen joint
slurping noodles
reading Bukowski
sipping a hipster cocktail
poems near the end of his life
I'm at the end of this life
the suburban life
the conventional life
I did it
got more shit than I know what to do with
good looking wife

good kid
big house
all so I can sit in this hipster ramen joint
drinking a hipster cocktail
wishing I was wandering the streets
or wandering through my tormented mind
like the poets
of old

Bitter

all I want is the brunette behind the bar
with slightly saggy tits
my wife is at the other end of the bar
laughing it up
with the neighbors' wives
I'm with the husbands
all of us fantasizing about the brunette
and her blonde counterpart
I'm drinking straight whiskey
I have a job I hate
and a wife that loves me
more than I love her
so, I keep drinking
this town we live in sucks ass
too quiet
too green
full of wannabe hipsters
Dixie hicks
and New York chic imposters
but
this chick is driving me crazy
so I drink away my dysfunction
eyes glued to her tits

Hope

without you, there is not much left of me
then, you bore a child
a daughter
a sign, of sorts
so we stayed married
I know I don't deserve this good fortune
I don't deserve your love, your touch
I don't deserve a pair
of deep dark brown innocent eyes
continuously knifing my soul
to its core
what I've been through
what I've put *you* through

but, here we are
after the drunken nights out with strangers
the coke addicted redhead and her husband
the shyster
the chick with the big tits that hates her husband
the aging drunk that lives a double life as a psychopath
strip clubs and internet porn
making passes at other men's wives in front of you
cigar smoke
a fifth of whisky and Taco Bell
after midnight
I'm barely alive inside

but you and our daughter
seem to be doing well
so, things seem to be going ok
when you cancel out the person
I've become

Inflation

the stripper said
she would drop her panties
for 20 bucks
that never happened to me before
I thought pussy showing was illegal in this state
what I miss?
was I too wrecked with Covid at the time?
was I busy pretending to be a dedicated husband?
I threw down a 20
there she was
bare naked on stage
I thought about getting a lap dance
when she was done with her set
but I was afraid she would be forced
to put her panties back on
time to do the smart thing
take the rest of my money
and go home

Bayou Vacation

on Frenchmen Street
a bar half full of tourists
she's the lead vocalist and plays trumpet
her voice is a blend of Billie Holiday and Keely Smith
something classic
something that never fades
I get a beer at the bar and sit alone
I make myself believe
that everytime she looks out into the crowd
she is looking at me
she's got a pair of tits to beg for
and a set of thighs to hug you close
she passes the metal hat around
I tip enough to get a copy of the band's CD
she smiles, "thanks so much," she says.
I order another beer and a shot of whiskey
the New Orleans jazz music plays
a blend of ragtime and back country folk music
after their set, I go back into the afternoon air
light a cigar
and head back down Frenchmen Street
into somewhere
unknown

Mirror

there is this white man
looking back at me
he's goofy
doesn't dress well
not very interesting
vanilla
he likes to play golf, apparently
he can't dance
he lives in the suburbs
drinks Miller Lite on Sundays
he hangs out at the neighbor's house on Saturday
he's so funny
when he's drunk
and he loves football
away from the mirror
I've learned to hate myself
guilt is the real addiction
I can't escape from

A Childlike Love

I dream that my mom is calling me
to come inside for dinner
she stands at the door
so beautiful
full of life
her skin soaked by the fading afternoon sun
her black hair
perfectly laid across her shoulders
I run to her
give her the biggest hug
"what's for dinner?" I ask
"your favorite," she answers
she looks back
before closing the door
she stares at me
as I am today
I start crying
"I love you," she says, "no matter what, I love you"
and I almost see god
I almost feel god
in that moment
as the world burns around me
I let it burn
because I know I'll be safe
in her warm

dead
arms

Suburban Lowlife

in this big house
alone
curtains pulled up
I binge drink
I start off with a Bloody Mary
then, switch to Old Fashions
in between cocktails
I take tequila shots
porn blaring from my tablet
I sink into the couch
I pause for a few hours
sleep it off
then, go pick up my daughter
my wife comes home
unaware
we kiss
she makes dinner
I soak up the alcohol with pasta
It's pasta night
so I open a bottle of wine
do it all again
this time
with a competent referee
to look over me

Admirer

my waitress
evening black hair and vanilla silk skin
I sing her a silent love song
from afar

Glutton

I have a thing for fast food
cheap Chinese food
gummy candy
and cheap Mexican food
I keep worrying I'll have a heart attack soon
because growing up in religion
teaches you to fear death
fear is always a forgotten prayer away
"one Sunday morning," the elders would say "we'll all rise up!"
I'm just a functioning alcoholic
that likes fast food
maybe a little porn
here and there
I put the burger to my mouth
and think about praying
but I would be trying to prove myself
to someone
or something
that claims to know my heart
regardless
I guess I'll just hope
to see my daughter
in the morning

Jazz Music

there's a bar
somewhere close
somewhere in the city
where I want to be
a place where sex drips
from the microphone, drums, and trumpet
where cigar smoke fills the air
where I have a nice black sports coat
somewhere to calm my troubles
and maybe
gamble a little bit
I watch too many old movies
but, why not?
why can't this place exist?
because old movies no longer exist
because only old people
like me
like jazz music
as my grandfather would say
"time waits
for no man."

Turn It Off

so many things going on
in the world
lives lost
greed
I get newspapers delivered daily
so, I'm always a day or so behind
what I know for sure
is that one of two old decaying white men
will be president
hallelujah!
God bless America
again!
we're in safe hands
so they tell me

Loss

endless droughts
a thirsty earth
longs
for change

Park Bench Philosopher

I believe in nothing
call for nothing to change
I watch people go by
I write poems of what I see
sitting on land
built by slaves
I write a poem about that
I take a sip of my coffee
look at more people walk by
the lady walking her dog
the fit man jogging
the family walking their kids
all occupying the same plot of land
built by slaves
each not noticing
or unaware
of the black face
watching their every move

T-Shirts

they say you wear
what you want to be
we've been told to be
"successful"
you should focus
on outward appearances
I like t-shirts and jeans
but I get away with it at work
because I've become expert
at flying under the radar
or, working for organizations with leaders
that are ego maniacs
too involved with themselves to notice me
maybe a little of both is at play
then again
maybe I'll be a poet
or a novelist
or a yogi
yeah!
that's it!
those jobs that make no money
so I can turn my stomach
on stale beer
and cheap cigarettes

Learning

open wounds
full of salt and honey
heal
with time

Poop Hat

I had this knit cap I wore everywhere
I took it to my mother in-law's church one day
can't remember what for
I was Mr. Cool that day
or, at least, I thought I was
gonna show these Jesus Freaks
what a civilized urban black man looks like
one problem
I had to take a shit
now, taking a shit is nothing new
everyone does it, of course
but it was a new experience for my knit cap
I pull down my pants
sat on the toilet
and began to unload
it was hot, wet, and stinky
I got up, wiped, put my pants back on
I went to feel my hat in my back pocket
it wasn't there
I had this sinking feeling
sure enough
there it was
floating
in the hot, wet, stinky shit
I grabbed some paper towels

fished it out
and threw it away
back amongst the crowd, my mother-in-law asked
"where's the hat?"
against my better judgement I told her
she laughed uncontrollably
before the night was over
half the congregation knew about my poop hat
anger gave way to humility
I realized something gravely important:
never take yourself too seriously
because the poop hat will follow
everywhere you go

Conspiracy Theorist

when the AI aliens turn on us
in the shape of humans
I hope I'm at the bar
cable news will say
it's a conspiracy by the radical left
or manipulation by the fascist right
Twitter will literally break the internet
the bartender will run out the door
phone in hand
I jump behind the bar
and pour myself another drink
as Musk's spaceship takes everyone to Mars
what's left will be us
a bar of drunken idiots
too drunk to do anything
too full of atheistic indignation
to even care

Author Bio

Jaron (JD) Vail is a poet from St. Louis, Missouri, currently residing in Columbia, Missouri. He began his writing career after completing the MFA in Writing program from Lindenwood University in 2011. JD also authors a bi-weekly newsletter titled Notes from a Park Bench Philosopher which includes short, sophisticated ramblings on a variety of topics. You can find JD and the newsletter on Facebook or email JD @ poet.prose2019@gmail.com